Summary

OF

Dare To Lead

Growth Academy

Contents

INTRODUCTION

This book is a summary of the famous book 'Dare To Lead', written by Growth Academy.

This summary is written for the busy readers to gain the knowledge and wisdom offered in the original book. It offers all the key concepts, ideas and examples to enrich the understanding of readers.

This summary guide of 'Dare To Lead' will certainly be a great help to understand the following:

- ❖ The myths about workplace culture and leadership
- ❖ The vulnerable nature of leaders, change makers and culture shifters
- ❖ How to cultivate braver leadership using the four skills set
- ❖ The seven behaviours that cultivate trust in relationships
- ❖ The findings of Brene Brown including her 20 years research and 7 years coaching

The book has everything that a summary reader wants, and our hard work and thorough process stands behind its quality.

BRAVE LEADERS AND COURAGE CULTURES

While penning down this book, Breene had a solitary goal in her mind:

"I earnestly want to share with you everything I've learnt over the course of two decades of working with hundreds of organizations; I want to combine my extensive research and countless experiences to compile a practical, actionable book on what it takes to be a daring leader."

She calls her goal the simplest and most selfish goal she has had.

Why selfish, you might ask?

Well, because she wanted to be a leader herself. She longed to live in a world populated with daring and courageous leaders and also wanted future generations to inherit and enjoy such a world too.

As per her books, a leader is someone who considers it a responsibility to perceive potential in people and processes and musters the courage to develop that potential.

As for what this book is all about? It consists of:

- ❖ The data gathered from interviews conducted over the past two decades
- ❖ The new research on the future of leadership

❖ The research based on the program evaluation of Brave Leaders, Inc.

Each facet of this book, whether an idea, concept or philosophy, is simple and straightforward. Yet, none are easy to implement. And why, you may ask, is that the case?

They all need courage, patience and perseverance.

The hindrances in the path of effective and daring leadership are rendered powerless if we show up, identify the barriers, and keep our morale high and curiosity intact.

To succeed, remember: what stands in the way becomes the way.

All the interviews started with one simple question: "What is it about the leadership process today that needs to change in order for leaders to be successful, despite the numerous challenges and a relentless demand for innovation?"

To our surprise, every leader gave a similar answer: To win, we need courageous cultures.

The author wanted to understand the reason behind this collective consensus for a call for a brave culture. However, out of the 50+ answers she received as a reply to her 'why' question, none of them actually addressed the question of courage.

She decided to ask them about the necessary skills that acted as prerequisites to brave leadership. This was a tough question to answer since less than half considered courage to be a trait rather than a skill.

A person may or may be in possession of certain skills but when asked, more than 80% leaders were unable to list skills that could indicate whether a leader is courageous or not.

However, she did manage to compile ten behavioural and cultural issues that most leaders identified as barriers to brave leadership:

- ❖ We tend to avoid difficult conversations that provide critical and constructive feedback
- ❖ We squander a significant part of our time in managing problem behaviours
- ❖ We do not work to foster empathy and build connection, leading to a lack of trust
- ❖ We do not take smart risks in response to market changes
- ❖ We get hung up on failures, setbacks and disappointments and thus, waste precious time and energy to no avail
- ❖ We resort to blaming and shaming instead of demonstrating accountability and learning from mistakes
- ❖ We are afraid to talk about diversity and inclusivity
- ❖ We respond to problems by implementing ineffective and unsustainable solutions
- ❖ We measure organizational values in terms of aspirations instead of valuable lessons
- ❖ We miss out on opportunities to learn and evolve due to falling prey to fear and perfectionism

Subsequent to the above realizations, the author wanted to identify the skills and qualities that would resolve the myriad issues listed above. Therefore, she conducted interviews only to find answers that were tested repeatedly.

The Heart of Daring Leadership

1. Only those who have the ability to be vulnerable can have the ability to become daring. Since courage and fear are not mutually exclusive emotions, simultaneously experiencing bravery and fear is normal.

The author was fortunate to discover that courage is an amalgamation of four skills

- ❖ Practicing vulnerability
- ❖ Living according to our values
- ❖ Promoting trust
- ❖ Learning to rise

The first step, which also functions as a precursor to the other three steps, is to practice vulnerability since the capacity for brave leadership is directly proportional to the potential for embracing vulnerability.

Self-awareness and self-love are of paramount importance since who you are is how you lead. Brave leaders have a heroic response to fear. An individual who conducts himself well has a greater chance to lead others well. If you treat yourself with patience and compassion in a time of fear or difficulty, then your response to fear is your strength, not an obstacle.

Remember, courage is contagious. If you want to build a courageous culture, then you need to do away with insecurities, restrictions and impediments and instead, cultivate an ecosystem where driven leaders, difficult conversations and passionate work is promoted.

Part One

RUMBLING WITH VULNERABILITY

Section 1

THE MOMENT AND THE MYTHS

The author recalled a moment when she was narrated a quote from Roosevelt. She learnt three most valuable lessons from that quote.

The first lesson is known as 'the physics of vulnerability' as she calls it. This lesson presents the fact that failure is unavoidable even if we act bravely. So, the most daring and courageous thing is to put all your efforts in a certain task even though you fear that you'll fail.

The second lesson states vulnerability as a feeling that we all commonly experience during hard times of uncertainty and risk. It has never been about losing or winning, but it's all about trying and making an effort when the outcome is uncertain and you have no control over it.

The last lesson is a binding rule, which she and her family residing over there sticks to. It says do not listen or take feedback from a person who is not daring enough to stand by the warfield and get his ass kicked.

The world is full of people who do not have enough courage to fight yet they boldly and confidently advise others especially those who're actually fighting.

You can easily recognize them as they are always offering their worthless feedback and unsought contributions based on criticism and fear. In reality, this happens because they have always been dubious throughout their lives and want you to be like them. This is a form of justification for their negative instincts.

Also if you focus on what others think of you and you believe that, you can never defeat your inner weaknesses. So, the best thing to do is to just ignore such people's advices and concentrate on what's really important to you.

But, at the same time, you need to be in touch with those whose opinions matter. Once you grasp this phenomenon, the next big question is how to find these true people in your life. .

To be honest it is easy to find such people as they are the ones who love you unconditionally despite all of your imperfections or flaws. These people will be true to you regardless of whatsoever the circumstances are. However, this list will be a little short as not many people can prove to be your true connections.

The Six Myths Of Vulnerability

The author believes there are six types of myths that actually tend to delude human behaviour regardless of their ability, age, country, culture, gender and caste.

Myth # 1- Vulnerability is Weakness

Vulnerability can actually never be the weakness. It coincides with courage. When the author asked the audience to give an example in which courage prevailed without vulnerability be it an engineer, teacher, doctor, CEO, athlete or any other professional, nobody was able to negate the aforementioned statement. This verified the author's statement.

Myth # 2- I Don't do Vulnerability

This is impossible because every action in our daily lives is surrounded by fear and unpredictability. Each one of us is victim to this phenomenon. What we can do to save ourselves from unwanted situations is that we choose our own vulnerability and deal with it purposely instead of it surpassing us. In this way, we will get a grasp on how to control our emotions and will be able to drive our behaviour and reasoning accordingly.

Myth # 3- I can go it Alone

Humans can never be independent and solitary when it comes to doing things. We are not meant to be grown this way. In fact, we should emerge in a way that others could rely on us.

Myth # 4- You can engineer the uncertainty/discomfort out of vulnerability

The reality is that nobody has ever been able to do itand there is no technology in this world that can help you gain it. So, to be exact and precise, you have to be courageous in vulnerability if you want to survive.

And the bad news is that if you try removing the unpredictability aspect of vulnerability you will run out of courage very soon. Therefore, the most effective way outlive vulnerability is to work on the four skill sets that actually help you build courage and grow with it.

Myth # 5- Truth comes before vulnerability

Trust and vulnerability have an uncommon relation. As humans we need to have trust to be vulnerable. And at the same time we need to be vulnerable in order to develop trust. Also, like all other complicated processes, both building trust and dealing with vulnerability takes time and drains our efforts.

Myth # 6- Vulnerability is disclosure

Vulnerability is a form of concealment.. Readers will either agree from the workings of the book that the six myths of vulnerability do in fact impact us or they'll just neglect the conclusions of the author holding on to their own beliefs and values regarding the concept of vulnerability.

In either case, whichever approach readers choose they might lead themselves to an eventual downfall. So, it's advisable that readers proceed with caution while choosing either of the two.

Vulnerability is, in fact, the core of all the emotions that humans try to keep away from. Therefore, the author believes that if one feels, he is vulnerable.

It is vulnerability that encourages innovation and imagination because until and unless we believe the true vulnerable nature of the innovation process we can never be creative enough to cause any significant change in the world.

However, if you logically think about vulnerability, you will find that it's a blessing in hiding. Vulnerability has gifted humans with many helpful skills, some of which are:

- ❖ Recognition
- ❖ Problem solving
- ❖ Decision making
- ❖ Feedback
- ❖ Hard work
- ❖ Tough conversations
- ❖ Adaptability

Section 2

THE CALL TO COURAGE

One single element that increases productivity and efficiency a great deal in every task we do or consider is 'clarity'.

The author credits all the successes she and her team were able to garner to the 'clarity' they had in their work. She says that the effect clarity can have on situations is simple but also transformative.

Throughout her career whenever she researched she always found out how much clarity has affected people, overtime, in the way they bond with others Even though she came across this ruling some 20 years ago, she didn't register it in her mental diary. Now, when she was finally considering it, her team gave her a negative response regarding clarity in communication.

Actually, in order to make her colleagues feel comfortable she used to share partial information and hide some of the expectations she had from them. In reality, she just wanted to be fair and frank with them. But, this plan didn't work for her. In the end of each process when they were answerable to her for the work, their performance lagged behind due to uncertain expectations.

The author found the same problem in other workplaces when she researched. She found out that many people avoid being clear about certain things so that they don't pose themselves as unfair or unkind.

However, she deduced from her findings that in reality it works differently. If you are being ambiguous to someone, you are increasing the chances for them to consider you as unjust and unpleasant.

The author was clever enough to soon realize that it was her fear and not a glitch in her management or goal-setting skills that led to failure of her business projects. She also realized that she was under a major influence of her emotions of terror and scarcity.

In addition to it, she also had long term goals and other obligations in her mind that she never expressed in front of her team. And these mental things were causing all the haste and communication problems in her business projects .

Had she shown some courage and trust, all of her communication barriers would have been removed and her team would have been in line with her vision and mission statement. She could have easily aligned her communication goals with her organizational goals . Remember, it takes real courage and strong faith to become a successful leader and lead by example.

According to her research, when people fear something, they should protect themselves too. For this reason, the author feels a need for people to use armour for their protection. The most common ways of using armour are:

- ❖ I am not enough.
- ❖ If I stay honest then it can be used against me
- ❖ If nobody is honest then why should I be?
- ❖ Why should I care when others are not honest about their issues.
- ❖ Their issues are the reason for my failure.

- I'm way better than them.

She relates the exercise of becoming a courageous leader with the treasure hunting. So, as a leader, she set out to hunt for her treasure.

She sought less of the following treasures:

- Fear of failure
- The scarcity mindset
- The anxiety of being alone

And she looked more of working together, towards the common goals which is both inspiring and exciting for all the team members.

The author narrates a story of Colonel DeDe HAlfhill. She had w over 33,000 officers under her command, not only did she teach them the power of serving others but also the wisdom behind this cause.

She taught her troops about the concept of inclusion. As a leader, she instilled into her followers a sense of building relationships and connecting with others when feeling lonely or disconnected.

She also told them not to call themselves 'disconnected', they'd rather call themselves 'lonely'. She did this because 'lonely' implies greater understanding of the most usual human feelings, especially in military where emotions like empathy, loneliness and compassion are not talked about explicitly.

Even though she feared that others won't like her way of connecting with her team, she went on with her idea because she knew it would be impactful on her team. She also resolved to research about the 'humanness' facet of leadership.

Although this was specified in the recent leadership manual, it is was quite undervalued, because of which she had to dig deeper and find the previous documents of military training.

She was surprised to see that all the words and ideas that were used to guide others have been altered in the recent training manual, making them less inclined towards human feelings.

To be an effective leader, you must have the dedication and passion to be and to do what it takes to be an inspiring leader. Otherwise, you can never relate with them on an emotional as well as moral level.

Section 3

THE ARMORY

Jobs before used most of our physical strengths, jobs right now consume our brain power but jobs in the future will require us to be good at controlling our emotions.

To love or to be loved is the most amazing thing humans experience. We tend to develop our personal security measures based on how much we're loved. We shield our emotions and hide our feelings in our quest to become emotionally strong.

One way to become emotionally strong is to merge our reasoning and feeling, widely known as wholeheartedness. The main plan is to combine them by detracting our armour and accepting every emotion that is related to our past and that exhausts our inner peace. We must acknowledge that we are chaotic and complicated people. It's a matter of being free and in danger .

It's easy to say than to do living with such form of wholeheartedness. . In fact, many organizations reward employees for their emotional strength, professional behavior and wholeheartedness. It helps them connect with people easily.

The harsh reality is that we harm our courage when we crush our emotions. In the process of gaining control, we actually lose it and the world starts to fall apart.

The most critical emotion is shame. It makes us doubt ourselves as if we are not worthy of connecting with others. It's such a strong feeling that it can easily trigger other negative emotions within us. Finally, our hearts act as our biggest weakness or vulnerability.

At the same time, our hearts can be our most precious asset if we wholeheartedly let go of our ego and other adverse emotions. We can easily then connect with others and gain others' trust and become phenomenal leaders.

The author gives 16 ways how armoured leadership acts and the relevant solutions courageous leaders presents:

Way # 1
Drives Perfectionism and Fostering Fear of Failure

We think that being perfect and doing tasks with perfection can save us from troubles and getting defamed. But it's believed that nobody's perfect therefore it's futile to spend our energy and time on trying to be perfect. Also, it becomes monotonous because we regard imperfection as something that brings us blame, shame and unnecessary judgements.

Encouraging/Modeling healthy, striving, empathy and self-compassion.

There is a slight difference between striving to be excellent and being perfect. As a team, we need to work in a certain direction that we don't get victim to the lust for perfection.

Way # 2
Working from Scarcity and Squandering Opportunities for Joy and Recognition

Joy brings with itself a certain touch of vulnerability. As humans, we hate to feel vulnerable, so we foreshadow joy and go for some self-protection.

This is the reason why we don't usually rejoice over small successes thinking to save it for someday in the future when big things come under our roof.

Practicing Gratitude and Celebrating Milestones and Victories

Practicing gratitude is a turning point. It lets us feel joyous over our victory without getting vulnerable at the same time.

When someone practices gratitude he gets to know what being victorious feels like. Yet he doesn't explicitly get involved in the celebration nor does he feel self-satisfied.

It elevates engagement, gratification and retention among the organization's employees because once they experience the feeling of victory they can't help getting addicted to it.

Way # 3
Numbing

Getting numb to different feelings and emotions is risky. It actually becomes like an obsession, if it's done continuously because humans can not choose what they have to feel numb about. It's either done comprehensively or not done at all. For instance, if we numb the emotions such as pain and discomfort, we have to numb the positive emotions of joy and happiness as well.

Setting Boundaries and Finding Real Comfort

The most effective solution is to set limitations, build the tools and discover real comfort instead of 'shadow comforts'.

The author considers our daily relaxing activities like relishing food, watching TV and others as shadow comforts.

We should set strategies and restrictions to aid the healthy rumble and find real comfort by connecting with others. This will boost the morale, efficiency, contribution and emotional fulfillment of the whole team.

Way # 4
Propagating the False Dichotomy of Victim or Viking, Crush or be Crushed

We are brought up in a double-edged world. We are made to think either in terms of winning or losing, yes or no, and right or wrong. Therefore, we are taught to crush others because if we won't eventually we will have to suffer.

Practicing Integration- Strong Back, Soft Front, Wild Heart

We need to bring all of our aspects together as we're not made of either positive or negative but both. At the same time, we must have a positive approach and grounded confidence while we accept our vulnerabilities and stand firm with unwavering courage.

Way # 5
Being a Knower and Being Right

We feel the need to be known as a Knower when we are shamed. In order to keep away from shame, having perfect knowledge of everything can help us progress in our relationships. However, this armour is defending in prospect and it appeals more adverse emotions in our lives.

Being a Learner and Getting it Right

The author proposes three approaches of mind shifting that a courageous leader can use. First, use your critical thinking skills and intuition to understand the issue at hand. Second, polish your learning skills. Third, urge asking the right questions to shift from 'being right' to 'getting it right'.

Way # 6
Hiding Behind Cynicism

Cynicism and irony both are methodical and accepted globally because they are directed towards the other person instead of the one who did it.

Modeling Clarity, Kindness and Hope

The three solutions to get rid of these issues are:

2. Stay clear and kind
3. Have courage to say what you exactly mean
4. Promote hope to negate despair caused by cynicism and condemnation

Way # 7
Using Criticism as Self-Protection

The armour of criticism protects the other person from fear or contemptibility, which reduce the likelihoods of innovation.

Making Contributions and Taking Risks

In order to survive the rumble, making invaluable contribution always helps. Also, people ought to provide thorough and precise arrangement with calculated risks in order to be successful.

Way # 8
Using Power Over

Those who want to inflict power and authority over others are those who have already been victims of unfair power in their past. But this only encourages opposition and defiance among others.

Using Power With, Power To, and Power Within

* ❖ Find mutual ground to develop collective strength, coordination and collaboration.
* ❖ Make others your confidantes with trust and confidence.
* ❖ And accept the dissimilarities and respect others' opinions.

Way # 9
Hustling for Your Worth

When we hustle for our value, we feel some authority over us and we tend to make more blunders. We try to pursue to gain importance in the eyes of others instead of serving them and earning the respect and co-operation that we deserve.

Knowing Your Value

The most effective way is to recognize and appreciate the worth of oneself and others.

Way # 10
Leading for Compliance and Control

If you see someone striving to get compliance and dominance, you'll notice that their driving forces are fear of failure or lack of authority. It negatively impacts creativity, imagination and collectivism. As a result, it becomes impossible to make use of the true gifts of people.

Cultivating Commitment and Shared Purpose

Create a culture where commitment and shared goals are common and co-exist together.

Way # 11
Weaponizing Fear and Uncertainty

Many leaders use terror and ambiguity to dominate their teams and to manipulate the way they work.

This behavior of dealing with the team helps in the short run with simpler problems at hand, however, when dealing with long term and complex issues it tends to get rough.

Acknowledging, Naming and Normalizing Collective Fear and Uncertainty

Uncertainty and Scarcity

Bold leaders communicate and recognize the probable occurrence of uncertainty and scarcity. It makes them courageous and helps them gain trust of rest of the team members.

Way # 12
Rewarding Exhaustion as a Status Symbol and Attaching Productivity to Self-Worth

Nothing is worthy of adding to the status symbol. The more you pretend anything the worst it gets for everybody else involved.

Modelling and Supporting Rest, Play and Recovery

One way to create a culture of valuable contribution is to support and aid rest, play and recovery, without adding anything to the status symbol.

Way # 13
Toleration Discrimination, Echo Chambers and a 'Fitting-in' Culture

People want to be authentic, all the while communicating with others and enjoying the freedom. Therefore, it is dangerous to create a culture of 'fitting-in' or looking for the support of others at work.

Culture of Belonging, Inclusivity and Diverse Perspectives

Courageous leaders encourage a strong sense of belonging. They motivate individuals to contribute, applaud their good work and give importance to their opinions.

Way # 14
Collecting Gold Stars

A leader who focuses more on collecting gold stars can never promote a healthy work environment.

Rewarding Others

A brave leader gives rewards to others instead of keeping all the rewards for himself. The best strategy is to motivate others and their hard work instead of searching for gold stars for ownself.

Way # 15

Zigzagging and Avoiding

Some leaders want to stay away from discomfort and unhealthy disputes, because these can make them lose significant amounts of focus, energy and time.

Talking Straight and Taking Action

It saves a great deal of time and energy of courageous leaders and helps them face the problems all at once.

Way # 16
Leading From Hurt

These leaders want to be regarded as 'important' and 'always knowing' instead of someone who is learning and climbing the steps of success. Their opinion is to act and to be treated like someone who is perfect in everything and it's others who tend to be wrong; not them.

Leading From Heart

Bold leaders are more sympathetic and understanding. They respect human nature and they don't make unfair judgements. They actually accept people the way they are with all their flaws and demands.

Section 4

SHAME AND EMPATHY

Shame is the king of all the emotions. It is also called the 'never good enough' emotion because it makes us believe that we don't deserve the company of others. It triggers mostly when we take notice of our flaws, and eventually we feel as though we are not worthy of good things.

The author considers shame to be:

1. A general emotion that every human experiences unless he lacks sympathy and human interconnection.
2. So embarrassing that people are afraid to talk about it.
3. More impactful on those who talk less about it.

According to the author, shame is a poisonous emotion . Also, it is often confused with guilt or embarrassment. However, the difference between shame and guilt is . That of a person who feels bad about himself and the one who feels bad about his action. Out of the two, the former one is shame while the latter one is guilt.

One's self-obsessed behaviour is actually driven by shame. How? When a person think he's ordinary, he gets conscious of himself and doesn't want to connect with other people . This thinking gives way to shame, which starts to reside in the person's mind making him a victim of narcissism.

However, after thorough research and survey , the author deduced the following facts about shame:

- ❖ Shame must never be used to weigh ethics. Also, shame and empathy can never exist together at the same time.
- ❖ The negative emotions like nervousness , depression, violence are all end results of shame, while guilt causes the apology made after such behaviours.
- ❖ People believe 'I deserve to feel ashamed while I don't deserve to be humiliated.'
- ❖ If we know that other people also get involved in such things we don't feel uncomfortable and embarrassed as compared to when we thought we were alone in it.

The author also tells us how to spot shame in an organization. She listed down the strong indicators that eventually lead to shame, hence if the following exists in an organization, shame is bound to coexist:

- ❖ Gossiping
- ❖ Perfectionism
- ❖ Favouritism
- ❖ Discrimination
- ❖ Blaming
- ❖ Bullying
- ❖ Teasing
- ❖ Harassment

Remember, the existence of shame is more harmful to the dignity of any individual than any other thing.

The real cure for shame is resilience as nothing works like resisting shame does. But the relevant amount of resilience that is required is achieved through emotional literacy. You need to be witty enough to understand your own emotions and how they impact your decisions and actions. If you are able to understand yourself, you can be true to yourself while shame is hovering over your head.

The author presents empathy as an effective remedy to shame. Her offered set of solutions highly depend on the following five empathy skills:

- ❖ Understanding perspective of others
- ❖ Being non-judgemental
- ❖ Considering others' feelings
- ❖ Communicating an understanding of other people's feelings
- ❖ Being conscious of others

The author provides the following six barriers to gaining empathy:

- ❖ Understanding the difference between sympathy and empathy
- ❖ The application of gasp and awe
- ❖ The fall in power
- ❖ How to block and tackle
- ❖ Boots and shovel
- ❖ Comparison and competition

In order to get better at resisting shame, the author believes we should work on the following four aspects:

- ❖ How to recognize shame and understand how it gets triggered
- ❖ Build critical awareness

❖ How to reach out to others

❖ How to speak about shame

Always remember, everyone has their own understanding of shame. And even though its solution can be subjective it will always be centred on empathy i.e. the core of connection.

Empathy is something that can easily be learned, it's not related to genes that it will have to come from within you.

Section 5

CURIOSITY AND GROUNDED CONFIDENCE

What exactly is grounded confidence?

The author thinks, "It is the messy process of learning and unlearning, practicing and failing, surviving a few misses."

This type of confidence is definitely not common these days. Grounded confidence is more authentic, it's based on reality and self-awareness that is gained through exposure and certain downfalls rather than through boasting one's personality and ego.

It's very easy to fall victim of this fake type of confidence as it forms a good reputation without any reason. However, it's long term effect is so fatal that it eliminates all the energy, effort and will power. Conversely, grounded confidence always gives a boost in morale for a longer term.

The most effective way to gain grounded confidence is by exercising courage, bravery and admiration. It's a worthy rumble skill which you excel in with more practice and perseverance. Note, no perfection can be achieved without consistent practice.

Once you achieve grounded confidence you can deal with the most difficult situations successfully because then you know your strengths and weaknesses inside and out. To put it ina different way, once you know how to rumble with vulnerability and courage you can play with the most deadly situations and come out victorious.

Moving over, the author adds another significant ingredient to the recipe of gaining rumbling skills, i.e. 'curiosity'. Curiosity requires an individual to not only have grounded confidence but to be courageous as well, because when we face unexpected situations we tend to lose control over everything. In that circumstance it's impossible to fake confidence and stop ourselves from jumping to conclusions and being comfortable even with wrong answers.

However, grounded confidence is the 'real armour'. It aids the courageous leader to use 'curiosity' to get to the roots of the problem and solve it. He also has a tendency to take opinions and suggestions from his team mates to deal with the problem.

As a leader, it is your job to always look out for horizon problems when the rumble gets a little hard and be informed about the status quo of the organization.

Curiosity has a Demand

Before you become curious, you need to have proper knowledge and awareness about things, at least to some extent. Also, before you encourage others to be curious, you need to be open about some facts and figures with them. You need to collect your own knowledge, curiosity and courage to effectively influence curiosity and learning in others.

Daring leaders are more approachable and relatable

Why?

Because they expect their staff to be fully committed to the tasks they have been given. This can only happen when they connect to their staff at a personal as well as emotional level. As a result, it helps everyone to be open about their insecurities and be relatable to each other.

The Benefits of Tough Conversations

Tough conversations have benefits, that the author has made us familiar with. To name a few; tough conversations enable us to connect well with others, be committed, be courageous and be vulnerable. Among all of these benefits, the biggest is being able to discover and add things to the portfolio of the company that benefit and at the same time, remove those that don't.

It's easy to say than to do for many. But good leaders know very well how to develop strong connections on the basis of trust so they find it easy. The nature of these connections so favourable that it becomes easy to talk over sensitive issues on regular basis without any personal conflict. Infact, the more they do, the better their relationship gets.

Part Two

LIVING INTO OUR VALUES

The phrase 'living into our values' is simply a reference to the idiom walk the talk.

Courageous leaders have the following things in common:

❖ They invest their time and energy to understand and define their values.

❖ They do not just talk about their values but also live by them.

❖ Their thoughts, words, actions and behaviour- all are aligned with their values and beliefs.

❖ They know and accept that there is a cost associated with living with those values. And they are prepared to pay that cost.

The author wants to help us in this regard. She shares anecdotes and her personal experiences to help us understand our own values and the whole process of living by them.

STEP # 1
Define your values before you even think of living by them.

It's pretty straightforward. .

No human being can perform an act or do a task when there is ambiguity, whether it be any instruction, suggestion or a tactic. Similarly, we need to invest some significant time to understand and fix our values. Infact, we need to define or label them before we move ahead.

This step may require us to take help from our friends and family. But it's actually a worthy thing to do and is extremely mandatory for us despite the phase or circumstances in our life.

One useful way to deal with it is to double check if we have created a set of values based on the context or situation in our life. Because if they are not subjective and contextual then they do not define the situation and need to be considered over again.

STEP # 2
Assess your behaviour with regard to your values.

Moving ahead, , it's time to get practical and apply our values to our own behaviours. Our aim is to discover and assess three or four certain sets of behaviour: the ones that are in close proximity to our defined values and the ones that are not. This evaluation will give us a valuable insight into our behaviour.

The most effective way to use this activity is to rethink about certain moments in the past and evaluate the causes of the two types of behaviours. The causes can be classified into the ones that were aligned with our values and the ones that we are attracted to

STEP # 3
Use empathy and self-compassion

The two most important human facets of following our values are empathy and self-compassion.

We need our close one to understand our values. That close one must use empathy to motivate and urge our efforts in the right direction. This little act will mean a lot when a leader will actually live by his values.

Also, we need to have a compassionate approach towards our own values. We need to get hold of our values and prioritize them first before we expect others to do so.

The author divides this step into further sub-steps:

- ❖ Find your supporter who knows your values.
- ❖ Know the type of support you want
- ❖ Understand your self-compassion for your values
- ❖ Express your feelings when in consistency with your values

STEP # 4

The author believes that when someone gives or receives feedback, it gets difficult for an individual to stay close to his values. This happens because certain emotions jump in and play their part.

The author then asks you to refrain from giving your feedback unless :

- ❖ You cannot help the other person in order to improve.
- ❖ You don't have the capability to understand him
- ❖ You cannot play any part towards the solution.
- ❖ You cannot appreciate his efforts
- ❖ You cannot identify his strengths and leverage them
- ❖ You cannot talk on the issue without any blame or shame
- ❖ You cannot own your part of the process
- ❖ You cannot thank others rather criticize them

- ❖ You cannot talk about the opportunities at hand
- ❖ You cannot model the vulnerability and openness that you seek from others

STEP # 5

Likewise, the author shares her strategies of getting feedback from others.

- ❖ Encourage yourself to listen to others with filters
- ❖ Always find something of value and ignore the rest
- ❖ Consider it as a path to mastery

STEP # 6
Value of sharing values is huge.

Sharing values can enable a leader to open himself to everyone. As a result, people feel comfortable around him and will connect with the leader.

And when the teams working together can relate with each other, there is a mutual and favorable exchange of trust. The communication barrier narrows down and sharing and caring becomes a two-way thing.

Part Three

BRAVING TRUST

Before we look into the concept of 'braving trust' it will be helpful to take notes of what trust actually is and why the author has told us about 'braving trust'.

According to the author, the word 'trust' is best explained by Charles Feltman who says 'Trust is something that we choose to risk our vulnerability with, and that too at the discretion of someone else'.

Trust is a delicate topic to talk about. It can cause severe relationship problems if it's not managed properly. Also, our society and the way we've been brought up has trained our minds to consider this topic as adverse. As a consequence, our first reaction is to refrain from talking about this topic.

But courageous leaders know that talking about such delicate topics as trust can save a lot of time and energy in the long run. Also, if conversations are properly directed, have the possibility to make the whole team connect and relate with each other.

It also can make us avoid gossiping about others because when the work culture encourages people to talk smoothly and openly with each other then why would anyone want to talk about others behind their backs rather than talking with each other?

The author has also provided us with some precautions when talking about trust.

- ❖ The leader should consider conversation about trust as something important. It should not be viewed as something that we must avoid.
- ❖ The leader must guide and teach people who want to talk with each other, especially in the case of trust issues.
- ❖ The leader must be specific. His discussions must be precise and he must not rumble about this topic as it can help identify the root cause and work over it.

The author has also defined the seven different features of human behaviour that are important to develop trust. She named the list 'BRAVING' as it is easy to memorize and expresses the true nature of trust.

The most useful rumble skill 'braving trust' can be learnt and practised to excel in it. The author, again, shares her commonly used conversation guide 'BRAVING' which serves two major purposes at every stage of the trust building process:

1. Assessment of trust factor among the team members
2. Measurement of trustworthiness of an individual

Following is the BRAVING list with each factor explained:

- ❖ BOUNDARIES- Everyone must be aware of his boundary. And if a problem falls outside it or is ambiguous , it must be avoided.
- ❖ RELIABILITY- Everyone must know their roles, expectations and competencies so that they're reliable enough to be given any task.

- ❖ ACCOUNTABILITY- Nobody should feel any stress when admitting to his mistakes and making the due changes.
- ❖ VAULT- Nobody should share any information or knowledge that is not their own or has any stake in it. Every confidential information must be kept a secret.
- ❖ INTEGRITY- Integrity means two things. First, everyone must be allowed to practise their values instead of just talking about them. Second, everyone must be encouraged to do the right thing instead of having fun and doing the easy stuff.
- ❖ NON-JUDGEMENT- Nobody should be judged when they're asking for help.
- ❖ GENEROSITY- Every act of others must be seen through generosity and kindness.

Part Four

LEARNING TO RISE

Every leader knows that a winner is the one who is ready to risk everything. In other words, a winner can never win unless he is willing to risk falling because that is when he gets back up and makes a move.

Now the question arises, what elements or processes make anyone risk falling in the first place?

Well, it is not someone's resolution or positive attitude rather it's a skill-based courage i.e. a courage which is backed up by a rumble skill. That rumble skill is learning to rise.

Before we try to grasp this skill, let's think about the example of a skydiver. A skydiver never learns how to jump into air before he actually learns how to fall on the ground.

Similarly, we can never expect any leader to show bravery and risk everything unless he learns how to rise. Such is the significance of this rumble skill.

The author, based on her survey, tell us about her insights about those who risk falling. They are actually the ones who show the highest level of resistance . They know how to support themselves and show courage and resistance when they fall.

Therefore, she suggests teaching the art of rising up as part of the leadership training programs.

The author has also provided a process called 'Learning to Rise' that is divided into three parts. According to her, this process has all the inputs needed - language, tools and skills that can be put right into practice. The process is hard but it offers a lot of rewards and bounties in the end that will eventually make it worth the effort.

The process consists of:

❖ Reckoning
❖ Rumble
❖ Revolution

STEP # 1: THE RECKONING

This step makes us understand the 'how' of proceeding towards a downfall In this step, we must admit that we have an emotional problem to deal with. After this, we must not generalize our state of emotion and discover a quick solution in order to escape that feeling as soon as possible.

The quick fix solution generally includes offloading work where we unload our emotions onto others.

However, the actual learning starts when we actually try to understand the reasons behind our emotions, why are we feeling them. Remember this learning can potentially transform anyone into a winner.

The author advises us to do 'tactical breathing' instead of 'offloading'. This is the most effective tactic used for reckoning our emotions.

The steps to tactical breathing are:

- ❖ Deeply inhale to expand your stomach to the count of 4
- ❖ Now hold the breath to the count of 4
- ❖ Slowly exhale through mouth to contract your stomach to the count of 4
- ❖ Now hold the empty breath to the count of 4

This will calm your mind allowing you to manage your negative and other emotional reactions like stress or anxiety.

While breathing, the author suggests us to ask ourselves the following two questions:

- ❖ Is the amount of information I have allows me to freak out?
- ❖ Even if the information is enough, will freaking out really help?

STEP # 2: THE RUMBLING

Before we dive into this step we must understand the true operating nature of our minds. It is: to protect itself. Our minds need to feel secure at any stage or circumstance . And this is why it makes up things on its own in the absence of complete and accurate information.

The author then proceeds to explain the two major human behaviours that a winner must abstain from:

- ❖ SFD- It is Shitty first Draft or the first story that we make up when we are short on information. At this stage, our negative feelings like fear of failure and other insecurities come into play.

As a result, we mostly draft pessimistic stories in order to feel secure . However, a winner would show his courage here. He will share the right information and seek patience and support from his team members.

❖ Confabulation- It is also a fear based sharing of information. It involves telling a lie that we believe to be true but with so much confidence that it appears to be a fact or reality. This lie is mostly our own opinion, expectation or may be the missing information.

However, the winner would come up with the true story instead of doing the above two acts. He can use the following three questions, as suggested by the author to reach to the true story:

❖ What extra can I learn about the situation in order to understand it? How can I increase my knowledge and challenge my assumptions?

❖ What more can I learn about the people involved? What additional information or clarifications can help me understand the stakeholders?

❖ How can I know more about myself? What reactions, responses and impacts my feelings can have on others?

In order to rumble, the courageous leader needs to have courage and emotional literacy. The first two questions will require him to show some courage while the last will demand emotional literacy.

Knowing that both courage and emotional literacy are hard to decipher and apply, the author shares the Story Rumble. This story gives the most useful application in the process of Learning to Rise.

The steps used in the process are:

1. First set your aim and be 100% sure about the reason behind your rumble
2. What ingredients are required to engage in the process with open heart and mind?
3. What things can get in the way of showing up?
4. How exactly you will show up with regards to points # 2 and 3?
5. Build trust and commitment by sharing the permission slips.
6. Define and name all the emotions that everyone will face.
7. What and how to stay curious?
8. Define all the SFDs and the strategies of having someone rumble with them.
9. What these SFDs tell you about your lives- including connections, trust, culture and others.
10. Where do you need to rumble? What do you need to rumble?
11. What is the difference (the 'Delta') between the SFDs and the new information disclosed during the rumble?
12. What are the key learnings?
13. How can you utilize such key learnings?
14. How can you integrate these learnings into your culture and strategies?
15. How and when to schedule the circle-back?

The author also reminds us of a factual finding. If you own the story from the start, you will get the chance to write the ending as well. But if you refuse to own it, then it will harm you.

STEP # 3: THE REVOLUTION

Now what is a revolution?

It simply is a decision we make when we explain our elements of joy and happiness. We then use these precise definitions to get an understanding of what real success is for us.

This revolution is about keeping away from our armour and using our vulnerabilities wisely, living by our values and braving trust among others, and learning to rise before we consider risking falling.

The more courage a culture has, the more the chances of success. Therefore, the real dare is to create a culture of courage with grounded confidence and vulnerability.

THANK YOU

Made in the USA
Lexington, KY
20 May 2019